Swimming with a Manatee

By Pat Goldys

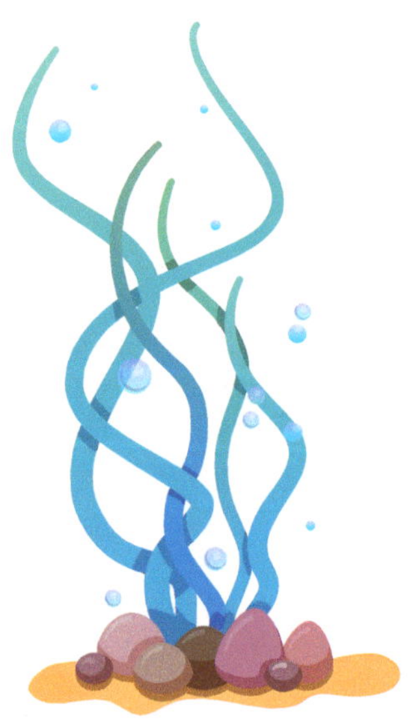

To Dani Pope, the best tour guide for swimming with the manatees.

To Victor and Christina, Natalie and Camilo and David and Chuck, who joined us on this wonderful adventure.

To Ryan, who drove the boat safely to see the amazing manatees.

Swimming with a manatee
I'm not afraid today.
These gentle giant creatures
Are kind when they play.

Swimming with a manatee
Is such a surprise!
Hold their breath for twenty minutes.
Comes to surface five times to rise.

Swimming with a manatee
I just keep looking to see
Split lips, head with hairy wrinkles
Using flippers to come near me.

Swimming with a manatee
I'm so happy to see
The barrel rolls and body surf
To entertain me.

Swimming with a manatee
I move at a slow pace
Not to bother when eating
Or touch their face.

Swimming with a manatee
I'm very excited!
Mama's baby is a calf
Who also was invited!

Swimming with a manatee
I just learned a lot.
Manatees are great mothers
Feeding and protecting on the spot.

11

Swimming with a manatee
I'm wondering and need to know
Why they move so slow,
Relaxed, never on the go!

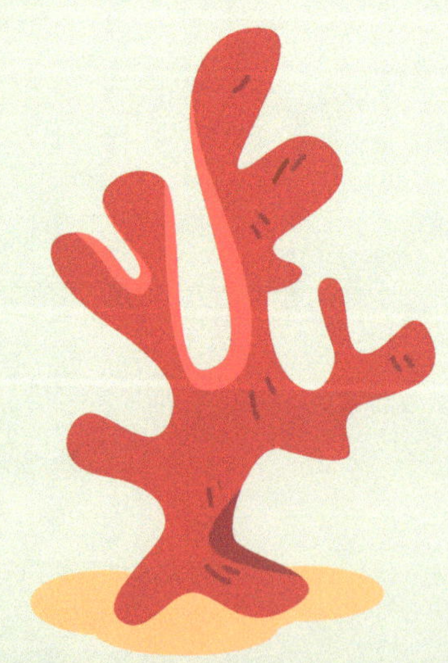

Swimming with a manatee
I'm looking for a friend
They are calm and curious
A whisker rub they will extend.

Swimming with a manatee
A smile I see.
Teeth are not for biting.
Because they are friendly.

Swimming with a manatee
Good morning I will say!
Just seeing this beauty
Will surely make your day!

Swimming with a manatee
Is a spectacle to see.
Egg shaped head, bristles everywhere
Big body coming towards me!

About the Author

Pat Goldys is a retired principal and grandma who always wanted to write books. When the pandemic came, the passion of writing children's books began. Pat is inspired by the children and the world around her. Her granddaughter reads every book, so it is kid tested. There are many adventures in Florida and they become the stories for the books! Pat loves nature, family, community, education and creativity. The books have lessons and imagination both adults and children enjoy.